WOLVE

What's inside?

- **2** World of wolves
- **4** Wolf alert
- **6** Timber wolf
- **8** Meet the family
- **10** Arctic wolf
- **12** On the hunt
- **14** Wolf pup
- **16** Leaving home
- **18** Back to the wild
- **20** Fast facts
- **22** Puzzles
- **24** Index

World of wolves

Wolves are wild dogs with thick, furry coats and sharp teeth. Most wolves live in families called packs. Together, they roam through forests and across snowy plains, far from towns and cities. There are two main types of wolves – grey wolves and red wolves.

red wolf

wolf pack

grey wolves

wolf pups

Guess what?
Red wolves are extremely rare. There are only about 300 red wolves in the whole world.

Wolf alert

A wolf is always on the lookout for other animals to eat for its dinner. Silently, a hungry wolf watches, listens and sniffs around, searching for a tasty creature to gobble up.

Sniff it out

Wolves have amazing noses. When a wolf sniffs the air, it can smell another animal up to two and a half kilometres away.

Look and listen

A wolf twists its ears to help it pick up sounds from every direction. What do you think this wolf can hear?

Guess what?
A wolf's fangs may grow up to seven times longer than your teeth!

Terrifying teeth

This scary snarl shows a wolf's powerful jaws and strong teeth. The four longest teeth, called fangs, are perfect for grabbing hold of prey.

Inside a wolf's mouth

Every tooth has a special job. Fangs grip food, while sharp front teeth cut through tough meat. Strong back teeth are for crushing bones.

Timber wolf

A timber wolf is a type of grey wolf that lives deep in the forest. Its grey, brown or black fur coat keeps it well hidden as it pads silently between the trees. A timber wolf hunts all kinds of forest animals, from small beavers to huge moose.

How fast?

A timber wolf is a champion runner. At top speed, it runs even faster than a cyclist whizzing downhill.

ha ha
How does a wolf say thank you?
Fangs a lot!

Timber wolf facts

At night, a timber wolf curls up on the ground and goes to sleep. When it's cold or wet, the wolf takes shelter in a hole where it stays snug and warm.

When a timber wolf spots a fish swimming in a shallow pool, it leaps into the water and snaps up the juicy snack.

Timber wolves are expert swimmers. They poke their ears and noses just above the water and paddle quickly with their paws.

Meet the family

A wolf pack includes a mother wolf, a father wolf and their young. The wolves in a pack play and hunt for food together. They also look after each other. But the parents are always in charge.

Know your place

When a young wolf misbehaves, an angry father wolf tells it off. The naughty wolf puts its tail between its legs and crouches down, as if to say, 'I'm sorry. You're the boss!'

Look at me

A mother wolf and father wolf are called alpha wolves. They fluff out their fur, prick up their ears and hold up their tails to show that they are the leaders of the pack.

Guess what?
Wolves have loud, spooky calls. You can hear their eerie howls up to 10 kilometres away.

What a noise!
Wolves howl to tell each other that dinner is ready, or to warn of danger. A loud howl can also help a lost wolf to find its way home.

First bite
At meal times, the parents eat first. The younger wolves wait for any scraps that are left over.

Arctic wolf

This wolf lives in the Arctic, a freezing cold place in the far north of the world. In summer, an arctic wolf has a greyish-brown coat. When icy winter arrives, this wolf grows a thick white coat that helps it to blend in with the snow.

How big?

An arctic wolf has enormous paws. It leaves prints in the snow that are almost twice as big as your hand.

ha ha
Why is a wolf like a stick of chewing gum? Because it lives in a pack!

Arctic wolf facts

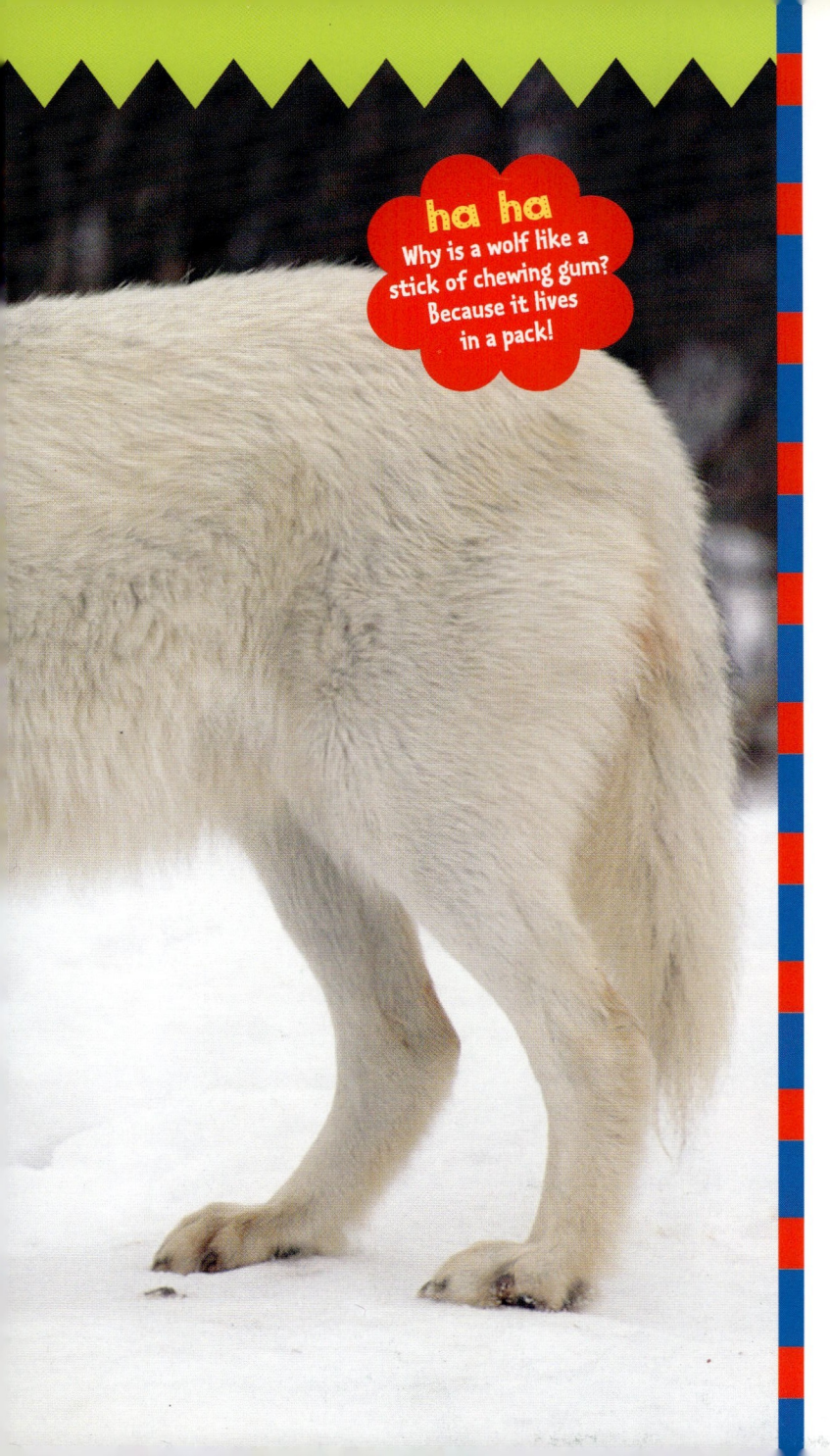

In the Arctic, giant blocks of ice float on the sea. An arctic wolf steps from block to block, taking care not to fall into the icy water!

When there's a snowstorm, arctic wolves keep safe and warm by curling up into balls. The snow quickly covers them and all you can see are giant snowballs.

Musk oxen make a yummy meal for arctic wolves. But oxen are strong and dangerous. When they see wolves creeping towards them, they prepare for a fight.

On the hunt

When night falls, hungry wolves go hunting. All the grown-up wolves take part. They hope to catch an animal big enough to feed the whole pack. This is what they do...

A filling feast

When wolves eat, they gulp down as much food as they can fit in their stomachs. Sometimes, they don't eat again for up to two weeks.

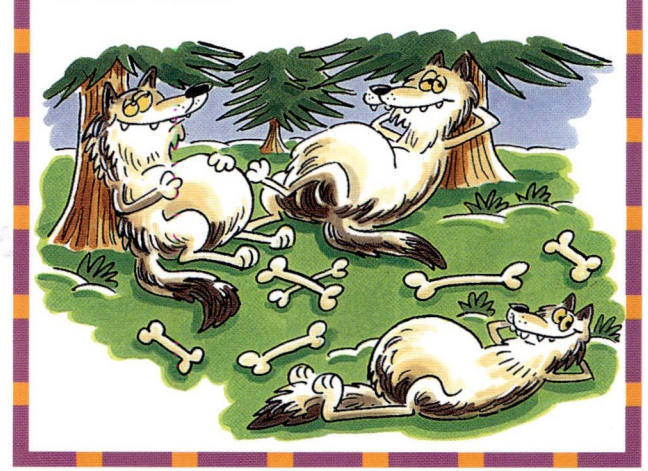

❶ Follow your nose

The wolves trot along, nose to tail. They sniff the ground, following the scent left behind by another animal.

12

❷ Hide and seek

Quickly and quietly, the wolves creep up on a moose. They mustn't let the animal discover them, or it will run away.

Guess what?
It may take a pack of wolves ten or more tries to catch a meal.

❸ Watch out!

All at once, the wolves dash out from their hiding places. But the moose runs quickly and this time it escapes!

Wolf pup

A wolf pup is born in a dry, warm place called a den. This may be a cave or a hole in the ground. At first, the pup snuggles up to its mother to drink her milk. Three weeks later, it steps out of the den, ready for its first adventure.

How small?

A mother wolf gives birth to about five pups at a time. The pups are so small that they could all fit easily into a shopping basket!

ha ha
What kind of clubs do wolves join?
Fang clubs!

Wolf pup facts

For six months, pups stay near their den. They play noisy games and practise being fierce hunters like their parents.

An older wolf chews up fresh meat for the pups to eat. A pup pushes its head into the older wolf's mouth and eats the mushy food.

When a curious pup strays too far, another member of the pack picks it up by the scruff of its neck and carries it back to safety.

Leaving home

A young wolf may leave its family to find a new home and start another pack. Or, it might be forced out because the pack is too big or because it has disobeyed the pack leaders.

Guess what?
A wolf may travel for up to a year before it finds a new home of its own.

Time to go
Pack leaders have a special way of letting a wolf know that it's time to leave. They bare their teeth and bristle their fur. Then the wolf quietly slinks away.

On the run

A lone wolf tries to keep away from other wolf packs. But if a lone wolf comes too close to a pack, the unfriendly wolves chase it away.

Thief! Thief!

One wolf cannot hunt big animals on its own. Instead, it catches mice or other small animals. A hungry wolf may even steal a chicken from a nearby farm.

A new home

In time, a lone wolf will meet a partner. They will have pups and start a new life together.

17

BACK TO THE WILD

Once, there were thousands of timber wolves all over North America. They lived in huge forests filled with tasty deer. Life was good!

1 Uh-oh

Then, about 100 years ago, people began to cut down the forests to build farms and towns. The wolves lost their homes and their food.

2 Hungry wolves stole animals from nearby farms. Often, angry farmers shot the thieves.

Not so fast...

3

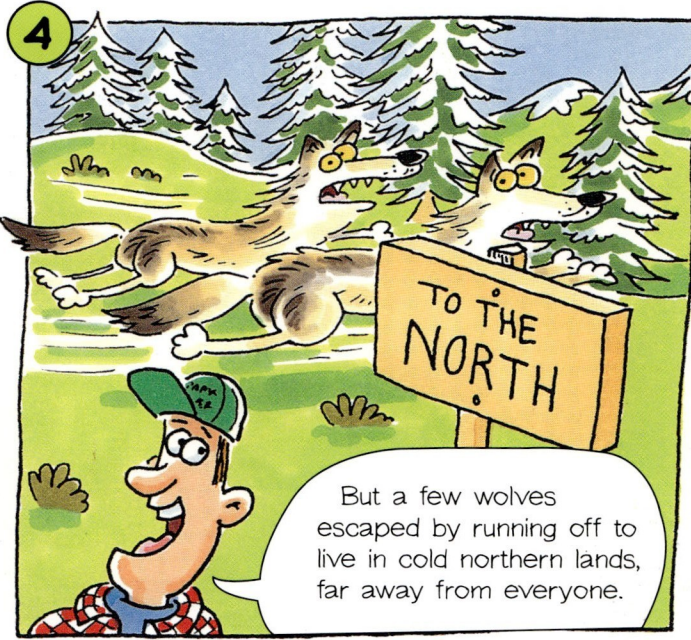

People also killed wolves out of fear. Most people believed that these wild animals were dangerous, even though wolves rarely attack people.

Was it something we said?

4

TO THE NORTH

But a few wolves escaped by running off to live in cold northern lands, far away from everyone.

5

Rescuers protected other wolves by keeping them in zoos. Soon, there were almost no wolves left in the wild.

NOW THEY'RE BACK!

Today, in North America, many wolves have been let loose in special national parks where they are safe to run free once again.

Fast facts

On these pages, you can find out more amazing facts about wolves.

Growing up

first day
A wolf pup is born. It can't see, hear or stand.

Timber wolf

Colour: brown, black, grey or a mixture of all three colours.
Home: forests all over North America.
Food: mainly deer, but also beavers or other small forest creatures.
Family: lives in packs of six to ten wolves.
Special body parts: timber wolves never look alike. Every wolf's fur coat has a different colour and pattern.
Amazing fact: a timber wolf is the largest wolf. It may be 1.7 metres from nose to tail. That's longer than you!

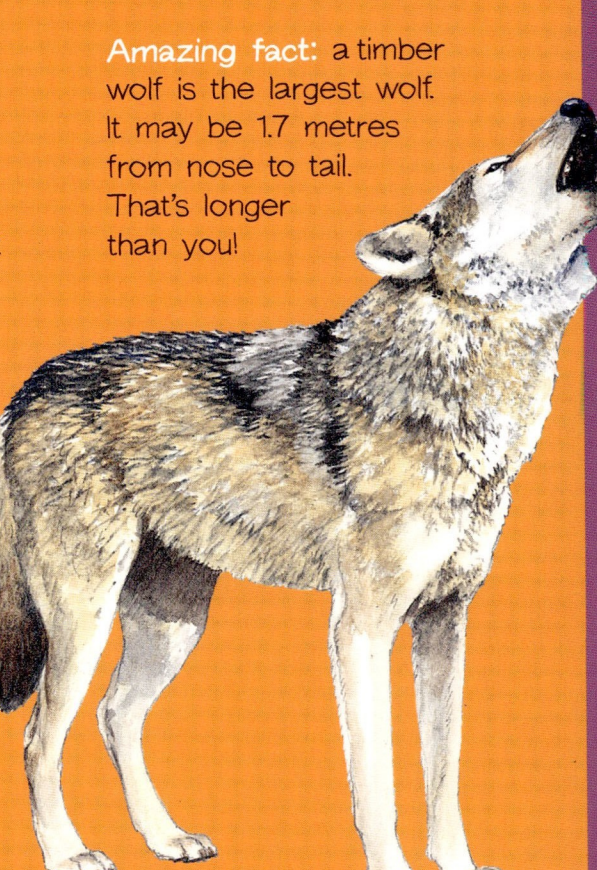

Arctic wolf

Colour: greyish-brown in summer and white in winter.
Home: snowy plains in the Arctic, a place in the far north of the world.
Food: musk oxen, moose, arctic hares or rodents.
Family: lives in packs of six to ten wolves.
Special body parts: extremely thick fur keeps this wolf warm and cozy in freezing cold weather.

3 weeks
A pup can stand and walk, but it doesn't go far.

2 months
A pup spends its time running around and playing.

1 year
A pup is fully grown. It has a thick fur coat.

2 years
An adult wolf is ready to start a family of its own.

Amazing fact: there's hardly anything to eat in the Arctic. A pack of arctic wolves may trek more than 19,000 kilometres to find food.

Red wolf

Colour: brown, grey or black with reddish head, ears and legs.
Home: the red wolf lives in mountains and forests in a small part of the USA.
Food: mainly small animals such as rats, rabbits and squirrels, but sometimes fish, too.
Family: these wolves often live in pairs or in small families.
Special body parts: especially long ears and legs.

Amazing fact: you'd be lucky to see a red wolf in the wild. Most red wolves live in zoos.

Puzzles

Here are some puzzles to try. Look back in the book to help you find the answers.

Close-up!
We've zoomed in on different parts of a wolf's body. Can you tell which parts you are looking at?

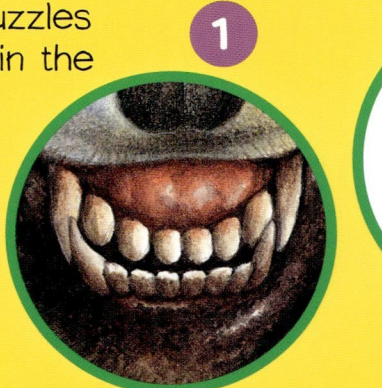

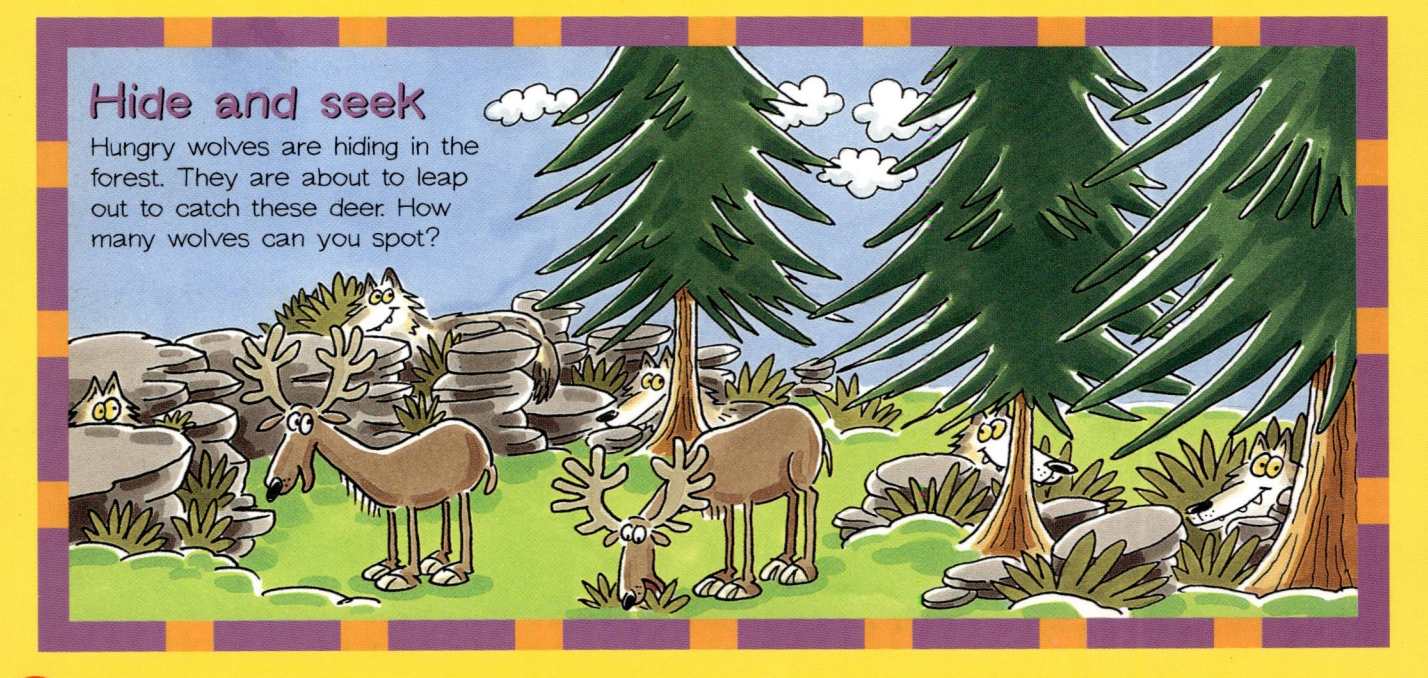

1

2

3

Hide and seek
Hungry wolves are hiding in the forest. They are about to leap out to catch these deer. How many wolves can you spot?

23

Answers
Close-up! 1. front teeth and fangs page 5, 2. ear page 17, 3. paw page 9   **Hide and seek** Five wolves
Spot the difference Picture b: moon is crescent shaped, there is only one wolf, the wolf's eyes are open, its ears are pointing backwards   **Track back** Timber wolf goes to the forest, red wolf goes to the mountain, arctic wolf goes to the snowy plain

Track back

These three wolves are trying to find their way home. Can you help them?

mountain   snowy plain   forest

timber wolf   red wolf   arctic wolf

Spot the difference

Look carefully at this wolf howling. Can you spot four differences between the two pictures?

a

b

Index

alpha wolves 8
arctic wolf 10, 11, 20, 21
den 14, 15
ears 4, 8
fangs 5
food 6, 9, 11, 15, 17, 20, 21
fur 2, 6, 8, 16, 20
grey wolf 2, 3, 6
howl 9
hunting 6, 12, 13, 17
nose 4, 12
pack 2, 8, 12, 13, 16, 17, 20
paws 7, 10
pup 3, 14, 15, 17, 20, 21
red wolf 2, 3, 21
teeth 2, 5, 16
timber wolf 6, 7, 20

Created and published by
Two-Can Publishing Ltd
346 Old Street
London
EC1V 9RB

Consultant: Anna Keen
Main illustrations: Eric Robson
Cartoon illustrations: Alan Rowe
Photographs: front cover Bruce Coleman/Hans Reinhard; p6 Liz Bomford/Ardea London Ltd; p10 Papilio Photographic; p14 Oxford Scientific Films.

Copyright © Two-Can Publishing Ltd 1999

'Two-Can' is a trademark of Two-Can Publishing Ltd.

ISBN 1-85434-791-8

Dewey Decimal Classification 599.74

Paperback 10 9 8 7 6 5 4 3 2 1

A catalogue record for this book is available from the British Library.

Printed in Hong Kong by Wing King Tong